DoD 5210.42-R

I0409653

NUCLEAR WEAPONS PERSONNEL RELIABILITY PROGRAM (PRP) REGULATION

June 2006

*Incorporating Change 1,
(11/10/2009)*

OFFICE OF THE UNDER SECRETARY OF DEFENSE (ACQUISITION, TECHNOLOGY, AND LOGISTICS)

ASSISTANT TO THE SECRETARY OF DEFENSE
3050 DEFENSE PENTAGON
WASHINGTON, DC 20301-3050

June 30, 2006

NUCLEAR AND CHEMICAL
AND BIOLOGICAL DEFENSE
PROGRAMS

FOREWORD

This Regulation is issued under the authority of DoD Directive 5210.42, "Nuclear Weapons Personnel Reliability Program (PRP)," January 8, 2001. It reissues DoD 5210.42-R, "Department Of Defense Nuclear Weapon Personnel Reliability Program (PRP) Regulation," January 8, 2001 (hereby canceled) and establishes requirements and procedures for the implementation of the PRP to select and maintain only the most reliable people to perform duties associated with nuclear weapons. Nuclear weapons require special consideration because of their policy implications and military importance, their destructive power, and the political consequences of an accident, loss of a weapon, or an unauthorized act. The safety, security, control, and effectiveness of nuclear weapons are of paramount importance to the security of the United States.

This Regulation applies to the Office of the Secretary of Defense, the Military Departments, the Chairman of the Joint Chiefs of Staff, the Combatant Commands, the Office of the Inspector General of the Department of Defense, the Defense Agencies, the DoD Field Activities, and all other organizational entities within the Department of Defense (hereafter referred to collectively as the "DoD Components"). It also applies to DoD military and civilian personnel and contractor employees assigned to PRP positions or in training for assignment to PRP positions.

This Regulation is effective immediately. Because of substantive changes, this Regulation must be reviewed in its entirety. Heads of DoD Components may elect to issue supplementary instructions deemed essential to the accommodation of requirements peculiar to their operations. Any such instruction may not conflict with the provisions of this Regulation. Any additional guidance issued by the DoD Components shall be forwarded to the address below within 30 days after publication and after each subsequent change for review.

Send recommended changes to this Regulation to:

> DATSD/NM, Room 3C125
> 3050 Defense Pentagon
> Washington, DC 20301-3050

This Regulation is approved for public release under unlimited distribution. Authorized registered users may obtain copies of this Regulation from the Defense Technical Information Center, 8725 John J. Kingman Road, Ft. Belvoir, VA 22060-6218. Copies are available on the Internet at http://www.dtic.mil/whs/directives/corres/pub1.html.

Dale Klein
Assistant to the Secretary of Defense for
Nuclear and Chemical and Biological Defense Programs

TABLE OF CONTENTS

APPENDICES

TABLE

REFERENCES

(a) ~~DoD Instruction 1215.19, "Uniform Reserve, Training and Retirement Category Administration," December 12, 2000~~ *DoD Instruction 1215.06, "Uniform Reserve, Training, and Retirement Categories," February 7, 2007*

(b) *American Psychiatric Association,* Diagnostic and Statistical Manual of Mental Disorders, *4th Edition*[1]

(c) DoD Directive 5210.56, "Use of Deadly Force and the Carrying of Firearms by DoD Personnel Engaged in Law Enforcement and Security Duties," November 1, 2001

(d) *United States European Command* Directive 60-12[2], "Nuclear Surety Management for the WS3 (NC)," June 1, 2004

(e) *Technical Publication 25-1,[3] "Department of Defense Nuclear Weapons Technical Inspection System," February 19, 2008*

(e/f) DoD 5200.2-R, "~~DoD~~ Personnel Security Program," January *16*, 1987

(f/g) Section 1408 of title 8, United States Code

(g/h) DoD ~~Directive~~ *Instruction* 5210.42, "Nuclear Weapons Personnel Reliability Program *(PRP),*" ~~January 8, 2001~~ *October 16, 2006*

~~(h) DoD Directive 5400.11, "DoD Privacy Program," November 16, 2004~~

(i) DoD Directive S-5210.81,[4] "United States Nuclear *Weapons* Command and Control*, Safety, and Security* (U)," August 8, 2005

(j) DoD 5210.48-R, "Polygraph Program," ~~December 24, 1984~~ *January 9, 1985*

(k) *Public Law 104-191, "Health Insurance Portability and Accountability Act of 1996," August 21, 1996*

(l) *DoD 6025.18-R, "DoD Health Information Privacy Regulation," January 24, 2003*

(m) *DoD Directive 5400.11, "DoD Privacy Program,"* ~~November 16, 2004~~ *May 8, 2007*

(n) *DoD 5400.11-R, "Department of Defense Privacy Program," May 14, 2007*

(o) *DoD 8910.1-M, "Department of Defense Procedures for Management of Information Requirements," June 30, 1998*

(p) *Security Executive Agent, Office of the Director of National Intelligence, and Suitability Executive Agent, Office of Personnel Management, Memorandum, "Federal Investigative Standards," December 13, 2008*

(q) *Director of Central Intelligence Directive 6/4, "Personnel Security Standards and Procedures Governing Eligibility for Access to Secret Compartmented Information (SCI)," as amended*

(k/r) DoD Directive 1010.1, "Military Personnel Drug Abuse Testing Program," December 9, 1994

(l/s) DoD Directive 1010.9, "DoD Civilian Employees Drug Abuse Testing Program," August 23, 1988

---

[1] Published by the American Psychiatric Association, 1400 K St., N.W., Washington, DC 20005

[2] This is a classified document. USEUCOM/ECJ5-T is the release authority for this Directive

[3] *Distribution authorized to U. S. Government agencies and their contractors as required by provisions of the contract for use in support of the nuclear weapons stockpile, as determined by the Joint Nuclear Weapons Publication System on January 1, 2007. Release authority is DTRA/CSN.*

[4] This is a classified document. DATSD(NM) is the DoD release authority for this Directive.

(m*t*) DoD Instruction 1010.6, "Rehabilitation and Referral Services For Alcohol and Drug Abusers," March 13, 1985

(n*u*) Section 1996a of title 42, United States Code

(o*v*) DoD Directive O-5210.41, "Security Policy for Protecting Nuclear Weapons," November 1, 2004

DEFINITIONS

DL.1. <u>Access</u>. Opportunity to tamper with or modify a nuclear weapon, critical nuclear weapon system component or positive control/Nuclear Command and Control (NC2) material. A person who is escorted by and/or under observation of *PRP-certified* individual(s) capable of detecting unauthorized actions is not considered to have access.

DL.2. <u>Active Service</u>. For assignment to the Personnel Reliability Program (PRP), active service is: active duty in the U.S. military; employment in the Federal Civil Service; employment by a U.S. Government contractor involving access to classified information under the National Industrial Security Program; continuous Federal service; service as a cadet or midshipmen in the Military, Naval, Air Force, or Coast Guard academy; members of the Selected Reserve as defined in DoD Instruction 1215.~~1906~~ *906* (Reference (a)). For PRP purposes, the following apply:

    DL.2.1. An interruption in active service of over 24 months constitutes a break in active service.

    DL.2.2. It is not the intent of this Regulation to allow repeated, short-term certifications into the PRP. Personnel must remain PRP certified while assigned to a PRP position in order to afford the certifying official the opportunity for longer-term, continual evaluation. Personnel must meet at the minimum, the standard outlined in section C4.2. if permanent duty assignments do not permit routine observations on a day-to-day basis.

    DL.2.3. Assignment as a Reserve Officers Training Corps, Merchant Marine Academy, and Maritime Academy cadet or midshipman is not considered active service.

DL.3. <u>Agency and Installation PRP Monitor</u>. An individual in the military grade of E-5 or above, or a civilian in the equivalent grade, appointed to administer and conduct oversight of the day-to-day functions of the PRP at DoD Agencies and installations.

DL.4. <u>Alcohol Abuse</u>. A maladaptive pattern of alcohol use as defined by the Diagnostic and Statistical Manual of Mental Disorders published by the American Psychiatric Association (Reference (b)).

DL.5. <u>Alcohol Dependence</u>. Psychological and/or physiological reliance on alcohol, as such reliance is defined by Reference (b).

DL.6. <u>Alcohol-Related Incident</u>. Any behavior to include misconduct or substandard performance in which the consumption of alcohol by the individual is a contributing factor as determined by the certifying official with consultation from the competent medical authority (CMA).

DL.7. <u>Access National Agency Check with Written Inquiries</u> (ANACI). A personnel security investigation *(PSI) conducted on a civilian employee* for access to ~~classified~~ *Secret* information conducted by ~~the Office of Personnel Management (OPM)~~ *an approved investigative service provider*, including a National Agency Check (NAC) and written inquiries to law enforcement agencies, former employers and supervisors, references, schools and credit check.

DL.8. <u>Armed</u>. Equipped with a loaded firearm. (See DoD Directive 5210.56 (Reference (c).)

DL.9. <u>Central Adjudication Facility</u> (CAF). A single facility designated by the Head of the DoD Component to evaluate personnel security investigations and other relevant information and to render personnel security determinations.

DL.10. <u>Certifying Official</u>. For military and DoD civilian personnel, the commander, or DoD military or civilian official, in a PRP position, responsible for nuclear weapons and/or NC2 operations having sufficient personal contact with all subordinate PRP personnel to permit continual evaluation of their performance and reliability. For DoD contractor personnel, the certifying official shall be the DoD military or civilian official designated in the contract.

DL.11. <u>Competent Medical Authority</u> (CMA). Must be a U.S. Military healthcare provider or a U.S. healthcare provider employed by or under contract or subcontract to the U.S. Government or U.S. Government contractor. They must be awarded regular clinical privileges for independent practice according to Service regulations by the healthcare facility responsible for the provider's place of duty, or if not privileged for independent practice, then be supervised by a CMA physician who is privileged to practice independently. Be specifically trained as a CMA and be appointed as a CMA by the medical treatment facility commander responsible for reviewing healthcare services or conducting clinical evaluations for the purpose of the PRP.

DL.12. <u>Continuing Evaluation</u>. The process by which a PRP-certified individual is observed for compliance with reliability standards. This is an ongoing process that considers duty performance, and on- and off-duty behavior, and reliability on a continuing and frequent basis.

DL.13. <u>Controlled Position</u>. A position, where an individual is assigned nuclear duties, which (see examples in Appendix 1):

DL.13.1. Has access, but no technical knowledge; or

DL.13.2. Controls access into areas containing nuclear weapons, but does not have access or technical knowledge; or

DL.13.3. Is armed and assigned duties to protect and/or guard nuclear weapons; or

DL.13.4. Has been designated as a certifying official at operational unit or staff activities with only designated controlled PRP positions.

DL.14. Counterintelligence Scope Polygraph (CSP) Examination. A polygraph examination in which the scope of the relevant questioning is restricted to specific counterintelligence topics.

DL.15. Critical Position. A position in which an individual is assigned nuclear duties where he or she (see examples in Appendix 1):

DL.15.1. Has access and technical knowledge; or

DL.15.2. Can either directly or indirectly cause the launch or use of a nuclear weapon; or

DL.15.3. Has accountability, control, or use of positive control materials or devices such as sealed authentication systems, permissive action link (PAL) materials and related codes, strategic and tactical nuclear-certified computer data (NCCD), nuclear targeting tapes or materials, emergency action messages, or release procedures for nuclear weapons; or

DL.15.4. Has been designated as a certifying official at operational unit or staff activities with designated critical PRP positions.

DL.16. Custodian. The commander of a U.S. custodial unit (*United States European Command (USEUCOM)*). Refer to USEUCOM Directive 60-12 (Reference (d)) for further detail.

DL.17. Custodial Agent. An individual acting on behalf of the custodian in maintaining control of access to U.S. nuclear weapons and maintaining control of weapons prior to release. Refer to Reference (d) for further detail.

DL.18. Decertification. An action based on the receipt of adverse information leading to removal from the PRP of an individual who has been screened, determined reliable, and certified capable of performing duties involving nuclear weapons. There are two types:

DL.18.1. Temporary Decertification. An action taken when the certifying official has information that could be expected to affect an individual's job performance or reliability and suspension is not appropriate.

DL.18.2. Permanent Decertification. An action taken when the certifying official has determined an individual no longer meets the reliability standards specified in this Regulation. When the permanent decertification is approved by the reviewing official, the individual will be removed from positions requiring PRP certification and the action shall be made a matter of permanent record.

DL.19. Disqualification. Prior to certification, an action taken based on the receipt of disqualifying information to deny PRP eligibility of an individual considered for, or in training leading to the assignment to, duties involving nuclear weapons.

DL.20. <u>DoD Personnel</u>. Active duty military personnel, members of the Selected Reserve, civilian employees of the Department of Defense or, for PRP purposes, DoD contractors and their employees.

DL.21. <u>Drug Abuse</u>. A maladaptive pattern of drug use as defined by Reference (b).

DL.22. <u>Drug Dependence</u>. Psychological and/or physiological reliance on drugs, as such reliance is defined by Reference (b).

DL.23. <u>Drug-Related Incident</u>. The wrongful use, possession, distribution, or introduction onto a military installation of a controlled substance, prescription medication, over-the-counter medication, or intoxicating substance (other than alcohol). (Wrongful means without legal justification or excuse, and includes use contrary to the directions of the manufacturer or prescribing healthcare provider, and use of any intoxicating substance not intended for human ingestion.)

~~DL.24. Entrance National Agency Check (ENTNAC). A Personnel Security Investigation (PSI) conducted in the same manner as a NAC.~~

DL.~~25~~24. <u>Exclusion Area</u>. A designated area immediately surrounding one or more nuclear weapons and/or systems. Normally, the boundaries of the area are the walls, floor, and ceiling of a structure, or are delineated by a permanent or temporary barrier. In the absence of positive preventive measures, entry into the exclusion area constitutes access to the nuclear weapons and/or systems.

DL.~~26~~25. <u>Healthcare Provider</u>. Any military or civilian provider authorized and/or licensed to practice medicine and to write prescriptions by Federal and/or State law or its equivalent if the individual received treatment outside of the United States. Treatment performed by healthcare providers must be reviewed by CMAs for PRP purposes.

DL.26. "L" Access Authorization. For the purpose of this Manual, a type of authorization granted by the Department of Energy indicating that the recipient is approved for access to the following levels and categories of classified information on a need-to-know basis: Confidential Restricted Data, Secret and Confidential National Security Information, and Secret and Confidential Formerly Restricted Data.

DL.27. <u>Limited Area</u>. A designated area immediately surrounding one or more exclusion areas. Normally, the area is between the boundaries of the exclusion area(s) and the outer or inner barrier or boundary of the perimeter security system.

DL.28. <u>National Agency Check (NAC)</u>. A PSI consisting of records reviews of certain national agencies, including a technical fingerprint search of Federal Bureau of Investigation, Identification (FBI/ID) files.

~~DL.29. NAC Plus Written Inquires and Credit Check. (NACIC). A PSI conducted by the Office of Personnel Management (OPM) that combines a NAC with written inquiries to law~~

~~enforcement agencies, former employees and supervisors, references, and schools and a credit check.~~

DL.~~30~~*29*. <u>NAC with Local Agency Checks and Credit Check</u> (NACLC). A PSI *for access to Confidential and Secret information conducted on contractor employees or Service members* covering the past 5 years and consisting of a NAC, financial review, verification of date and place of birth, and local agency checks. *This investigation is also used for reinvestigation for Confidential and Secret clearances on civilian employees, contractor employees, and Service members.*

DL.~~31~~*30*. <u>Nuclear Certified Computer Data</u> (NCCD). Nuclear certified media containing nuclear mission or launch control data.

DL.~~32~~*31*. <u>Nuclear Command and Control (NC2) Materials</u>. Materials and devices used in the coding and authentication processing and communication medium necessary to transmit release, execution, or termination orders; and nuclear weapons targeting tapes or media containing nuclear weapons targeting data.

DL.~~33~~*32*. <u>Periodic Reinvestigation</u> (PR). An investigation conducted at specified intervals for updating a previously completed PSI.

DL.33. <u>PRP Inspector</u>. A specifically designated individual performing in an oversight role who evaluates the PRP for compliance. He or she is selected by and reports to an organization in a PRP oversight role performing Nuclear Weapons Technical Inspections as defined in Technical Publication 25-1 (Reference (e)). Also applies to staff assistance and/or assessment visits.

DL.34. <u>Personnel Security Investigation</u> (PSI). Any investigation required for determining the eligibility of DoD military or civilian personnel and contractor employees for access to classified information, acceptance, or retention in the armed forces, or assignment to, and retention in, sensitive positions.

DL.35. <u>Positive Control Materials or Devices</u>. Sealed authentication systems, PAL, coded switch system, positive enable system, or NCCD material or devices.

DL.36. <u>Potentially Disqualifying Information</u> (PDI). Any information that may cast doubt about an individual's ability or reliability to perform duties related to nuclear weapons.

DL.37. <u>"Q" Access Authorization</u>. For the purpose of this Manual, a type of authorization granted by the Department of Energy indicating that the recipient is approved for access to the following levels of classified matter on a need-to-know basis: Top Secret, Secret, and Confidential Restricted Data, National Security Information, and Formerly Restricted Data.

DL.~~37~~*38*. <u>Random Testing</u>. A program of substance abuse testing where each member of the testing population has an equal chance of being selected. Random testing may be either testing of designated individuals occupying a specified area, element, or position, or random testing of those individuals based on a neutral criterion, such as a digit of the social security number.

DL.~~38~~39. <u>Reviewing Official</u>. The commander, or designated DoD military or civilian official, at a level above that of the certifying official, who is responsible for operations involving nuclear weapons.

DL.40. <u>Screening</u>. A process that includes a review of medical and dental records, personnel records, personnel security investigations, and other pertinent documents and/or information and a personal interview for the purpose of validating an individual's reliability to be considered for the PRP.

DL.~~39~~41. <u>Sensitive Position</u>. Any position so designated in the Department of Defense, the occupant of which could bring about, by virtue of the type of the position, a materially adverse effect on the national security. All civilian positions are either special-sensitive, critical-sensitive, noncritical-sensitive, or nonsensitive.

DL.~~40~~42. <u>Single-Scope Background Investigation</u> (SSBI). A PSI consisting of both record reviews and interviews with sources of information according to DoD 5200.2-R (Reference (*ef*)).

DL.~~41~~43. <u>Suspension</u>. An action to remove, or suspend, an individual from PRP duties when reliability is not in question.

DL.~~42~~44. <u>Technical Knowledge</u>. Knowledge that would allow an individual to perform an intentional act on a nuclear weapon, a critical nuclear weapon system component, or positive control/NC2 material in a manner that could go undetected during normal monitoring or operations and could cause the unauthorized pre-arming, arming, launching, releasing, disablement, or detonation of a nuclear weapon or degradation of weapon performance.

DL.45. <u>Tier 2 Investigation</u>. Investigations conducted to this standard are for positions designated as moderate risk non-critical sensitive, and/or to allow access to "L" information, Confidential information, and Secret information. This is the lowest level of investigation acceptable for access to classified information. Frequency: At least 20 percent of subjects in Tier 2 shall be reevaluated annually, with 100 percent being reevaluated at least once every 5 years and on a periodic basis or as event-driven, subject to implementing guidance.

DL.46. <u>Tier 3 Investigation</u>. Investigations conducted to this standard are for positions designated as high risk, critical sensitive, special sensitive, and/or to allow access to "Q" information, Top Secret information, and Sensitive Compartmented Information (SCI). Frequency: Subjects in Tier 3 shall be reevaluated annually or as event-driven, subject to implementing guidance.

DL.~~43~~47. <u>U.S. Citizen (native born or naturalized)</u>. A person born in one of the following locations is considered a U.S. citizen for PRP purposes: the 50 States, and the District of Columbia, Puerto Rico, Guam, American Samoa, Northern Mariana Islands, U.S. Virgin Islands, the Federated States of Micronesia, and the Republic of the Marshall Islands. Additionally, a person born to U.S. citizens living in a foreign country who has a U.S. birth certificate, a certification of birth abroad, or for whom a naturalization certificate is issued.

DL.4448. <u>U.S. National</u>. A citizen of the United States or other person formally designated as a U.S. national. Section 1408 of 8 United States Code (U.S.C.) (Reference (fg)) provides a detailed identification of non-citizen U.S. nationals.

AL1. ABBREVIATIONS AND ACRONYMS

ANACI	Access National Agency Check with Inquiries
ATSD(NCB)/NM	Assistant to the Secretary of Defense for Nuclear and Chemical and Biological Defense Programs, Nuclear Matters Office
BI	Background Investigation
CAF	Central Adjudication Facility
CMA	Competent Medical Authority
CSP	Counterintelligence-Scope Polygraph
DISCO	Defense Industrial Security Clearance Office
DSS	Defense Security Service
DoD	Department of Defense
EOD	Explosive Ordnance Disposal
IDC	Independent Duty Hospital Corpsmen
IDMT	Independent Duty Medical Technician
MACOM	Major Command, Army
MAJCOM	Major Command, Air Force
MUNSS	Munitions Support Squadron
NAC	National Agency Check
NACI	National Agency Check with Inquiries
NACLC	National Agency Check with Local Agency Checks and Credit Check
NC2	Nuclear Command and Control
NCCD	Nuclear-Certified Computer Data
OPM	Office of Personnel Management
PAL	Permissive Action Link
PDI	Potentially Disqualifying Information
PPR	Phased Periodic Reinvestigation
PR	Periodic Reinvestigation
PRP	Personnel Reliability Program
PSI	Personnel Security Investigation
SBI	Special Background Investigation
SPR	Secret Periodic Reinvestigation
SSBI	Single-Scope Background Investigation
TAD	Temporary Additional Duty
TDY	Temporary Duty Assignment
USEUCOM	United States European Command
U.S.C.	United States Code

C1. CHAPTER 1

GENERAL PROVISIONS

C1.1. PURPOSE

The purpose of the Personnel Reliability Program (PRP) is to ensure that each person ~~who performs duties involving nuclear weapons meets the reliability standards of the PRP~~ *selected and retained for performing duties associated with nuclear weapons or nuclear command and control systems and equipment is emotionally stable and physically capable, and has demonstrated reliability and professional competence*. This shall be accomplished through the initial and continual evaluation of individuals assigned to PRP duties. The management of the PRP is a function of command. However, each person assigned to PRP duties is responsible for their reliability and has an obligation to report to the certifying official any behavior or circumstance about themselves or others in the PRP that may be expected to result in degradation in job performance or personal reliability or an unsafe or insecure condition involving nuclear weapons and/or Nuclear Command and Control (NC2) material. The PRP supporting agencies and supervisors of individuals performing PRP duties shall assist the reviewing and certifying officials in their initial and continuing evaluation duties by ensuring that all PDI is made available for their consideration. This Regulation provides procedures for the implementation of ~~Reference (f) and~~ DoD ~~Directive~~ *Instruction* 5210.42 (Reference (~~g~~*h*)).

C1.2. PRP ADMINISTRATORS

C1.2.1. <u>Designation of Reviewing and Certifying Officials</u>. The Heads of the DoD Components shall establish procedures for formally designating the reviewing officials and certifying officials. The certifying officials shall be designated as critical or controlled PRP positions commensurate with the highest category of any nuclear duty position in the unit or activity concerned.

C1.2.2. <u>Designation of Competent Medical Authority</u> (CMA). The Heads of the DoD Components shall establish procedures to appoint an agency or installation CMA to act as a PRP medical consultant to provide recommendations to the reviewing and certifying officials on individuals' suitability to perform PRP duties.

C1.2.3. <u>Agency and Installation PRP Monitor</u>. DoD agencies, installations, and subordinate units with large PRP populations shall consider appointing a PRP monitor(s) as appropriate, to administer the day-to-day functions of the PRP. The agency or installation PRP monitor coordinates and disseminates PRP information to the reviewing and certifying officials, unit commanders, PRP monitors, and supporting staff agencies; indoctrinates and trains unit PRP personnel and administrators on program objectives and procedures; maintains the installation PRP roster; and conducts staff assistance visits to all subordinate units with a PRP.

C1.3. PRP POSITIONS

All PRP positions shall be formally designated as either critical or controlled and restricted to the minimum number required to accomplish the mission. Additionally, personnel selected for designated NC2 PRP positions according to DoD Directive S-5210.81 (Reference (i)), shall be subject to random Counterintelligence-Scope Polygraph (CSP) examinations administered according to DoD 5210.48-R (Reference (j)). Only certified personnel shall be assigned to designated PRP positions. When PRP positions become vacant, certified personnel shall be assigned as rapidly as possible. Examples of typical PRP positions are shown in Appendix 1.

C1.3.1. Critical Position. A position, where an individual is assigned nuclear duties where he or she (see examples in Appendix 1):

C1.3.1.1. Has access and technical knowledge; or

C1.3.1.2. Can either directly or indirectly cause the launch or use of a nuclear weapon; or

C1.3.1.3. Has accountability, control, or use of positive control materials or devices such as sealed authentication systems, permissive action link (PAL) materials and related codes, strategic and tactical nuclear-certified computer data (NCCD), nuclear targeting tapes or materials, emergency action messages, or release procedures for nuclear weapons; or

C1.3.1.4. Has been designated as a certifying official at operational unit or staff activities with designated critical PRP positions.

C1.3.2. Controlled Position. A position in which an individual is assigned nuclear duties where he or she (see examples in Appendix 1):

C1.3.2.1. Has access, but no technical knowledge; or

C1.3.2.2. Controls access into areas containing nuclear weapons, but does not have access or technical knowledge; or

C1.3.2.3. Is armed and assigned duties to protect and/or guard nuclear weapons; or

C1.3.2.4. Has been designated as a certifying official at operational unit or staff activities with only designated controlled PRP positions.

C1.4. TRAINING

C1.4.1. Heads of the DoD Components shall establish frequency of refresher training and further define and establish training requirements in Service directives. Reviewing officials, certifying officials, PRP monitors, CMAs and other medical personnel (e.g., *Independent Duty Hospital Corpsmen (*IDC*), Independent Duty Medical Technicians (*IDMT*))* who review PRP medical issues), and individuals assigned to PRP duties shall receive initial training, refresher PRP training, and be thoroughly briefed on their PRP management and oversight responsibilities.

C1.4.2. Initial and refresher training shall include, at a minimum:

C1.4.1.1. PRP purpose (spirit and intent).

C1.4.1.2. PRP roles and responsibilities.

C1.4.1.3. PRP certification.

C1.4.1.4. Continuing evaluation.

C1.4.1.5. Disqualification, removal, and reinstatement.

C1.4.1.6. Health Insurance Portability and Accountability Act and Privacy Act requirements in accordance with Public Law 104-191 (Reference (k)) and DoD 6025.18-R (Reference (l)), respectively.

C1.5. PRP REVIEW AND EVALUATION

C1.5.1. The Heads of the DoD Components shall ensure that the PRP is reviewed and evaluated during appropriate inspections and staff visits at all levels of command. The results of those inspections shall be reviewed periodically at the highest level in the DoD Component to ensure effective and consistent application of the PRP.

C1.5.2. Designated PRP inspectors, as defined in this Regulation, or staff assistance and/or assessment visit team members are authorized to review medical records of candidates and members of the PRP, and shall comply with Reference (l), which authorizes disclosure of protected health information for specialized Government functions. PRP inspectors that review medical records must be trained by methods established and approved by the Joint Staff (for Defense Threat Reduction Agency inspectors) and the Services (for Service inspectors) on health information review and Reference (k) requirements. Access is limited to those records and medical information associated with an individual's participation in the PRP Program. Questionable medical PDI discovered during inspection and/or review shall be referred to a CMA for resolution.

C1.5.3. Personally identifiable information (PII) collected and utilized in the execution of this program must be safeguarded to prevent any unauthorized use. The DoD Components shall ensure the collection, use, and release of PII complies with the requirements of DoD Directive 5400.11 (Reference (m)) and DoD 5400.11-R (Reference (n)).

C2. CHAPTER 2

ROLES AND RESPONSIBILITIES

C2.1. DoD COMPONENTS

C2.1.1. Develop and implement standards and procedures ensuring due process for individuals identified for disqualification or decertification under this Regulation.

C2.1.2. Are the final approval authority for reinstatement or requalification for individuals permanently decertified or disqualified under this Regulation.

C2.1.3. Establish frequency of refresher training and further define and establish training requirements in Service directives.

C2.1.4. Ensure all medical personnel have been instructed in the purpose of the PRP and have been advised of their reporting responsibilities.

C2.1.4.1. Medical personnel providing PRP support will be given an initial, and thereafter periodic orientation in nuclear weapons operations, emphasizing safety and security aspects and the responsibility for advising the unit commander of medical conditions that adversely effect the certification of unit personnel.

C2.1.4.2. There shall be close cooperation and coordination between the nuclear weapon organization and the designated medical support activity to assure continuing application of PRP standards.

C2.1.5. Ensure all security personnel have been instructed in the personnel security requirements for access to the nuclear weapons PRP and their responsibility to advise the certifying official and/or reviewing official of personnel security issues that adversely affect the certification of PRP members.

C2.1.56. Ensure a substance abuse testing program is established for all personnel assigned to PRP positions including contractor personnel as applicable. The extent to which PRP personnel shall be tested and the criteria for testing shall be determined by the Heads of the DoD Components.

C2.1.67. Ensure DoD criminal investigative agencies immediately notify the certifying official *and/or the subject's respective central adjudication facility (CAF)* of any individual in the PRP who is under investigation and the circumstances of the investigation.

C2.1.78. Ensure the PRP is reviewed and evaluated during appropriate inspections and staff visits at all levels of command. The results shall be reviewed periodically at the highest level in the DoD Component to ensure effective and consistent application of the PRP.

C2.1.89. Submit annual program status reports to the Assistant to the Secretary of Defense for Nuclear and Chemical and Biological Defense Programs, Nuclear Matters Office (ATSD(NCB)/NM) as described in Appendix 2. *The annual program status reports have been assigned RCS DD-AT&L(A)1403 in accordance with DoD 8910.1-M (Reference (o)).*

C2.2. COMBATANT COMMANDS

C2.2.1. Submit annual program status reports to the ATSD(NCB)/NM as described in Appendix 2.

C2.2.2. As applicable, provide initial and refresher PRP training, through briefings to certifying officials, medical personnel, PRP monitors, and certified individuals on their PRP management and oversight responsibilities.

C2.3. REVIEWING OFFICIALS

C2.3.1. Ensure the requirements of the PRP are implemented and all personnel comply with applicable standards.

C2.3.2. Review all permanent PRP decertifications.

C2.3.2.1. Following the review of a permanent decertification, notify the individual and certifying official of the findings and conclusion within 15 *work*days.

C2.3.2.2. In the case of a DoD contractor employee, ensure the contractor is notified that the employee has been decertified and must be reassigned to non-PRP duties.

C2.3.3. As necessary, review medical and personnel records. PRP reviewing officials are authorized to review medical records of candidates and members of the PRP to make determinations required by this Regulation. (DoDD 5400.11, Reference (h)). However, PRP reviewing officials may only have access to portions of the medical records where the CMA has identified a possible disqualifying condition. Access is limited to the extent necessary for the reviewing official to document the condition to make a certification/qualification determination for PRP purposes. *However, such reviews will be to the minimum extent necessary for the reviewing official to make a certification and/or qualification determination for PRP purposes.*

C2.4. CERTIFYING OFFICIALS

C2.4.1. Make a judgment on the reliability of each individual identified for PRP duties. This will be based on the appropriate personnel security investigation (PSI), physical and mental capability, a review of personnel and medical records, and a personal interview. See paragraph C3.3.2.1.3 for restrictions on access to medical records for certifying officials.

C2.4.2. Consider all relevant facts applicable to the individual's performance record, the recommendations expressed in the PSIs and medical evaluations, and the opinions of other agencies and personnel, as appropriate, to make the final judgment about an individual's reliability and whether he or she can be depended on to respond in a stable manner when performing PRP duties.

C2.4.3. Review medical and personnel records as necessary. PRP certifying officials are authorized to review medical records of candidates and members of the PRP to make determinations required by this Regulation. ~~(see Reference (h)). However, PRP certifying officials may only have access to portions of the medical records where the CMA has identified a possible disqualifying condition. Access is limited to the extent necessary for the certifying official to document the condition to make a certification/qualification determination for PRP purposes.~~ *However, such reviews will be to the minimum extent necessary for the reviewing official to make a certification and/or qualification determination for PRP purposes.*

C2.4.4. Conduct a personal interview of each PRP candidate. As a minimum, the personal interview shall cover:

C2.4.4.1. The significance of the PRP assignment and PRP standards.

C2.4.4.2. The need for reliable performance.

C2.4.4.3. Individual responsibility for self-reporting and peer review of factors and situations that could adversely affect job performance or reliability.

C2.4.4.4. The certifying official will also provide the individual the opportunity to disclose any PDI.

C2.4.5. Provide for the continuing evaluation of all PRP-certified personnel.

C2.4.5.1. Ensure that all military, civilian, and contractor personnel assigned to PRP positions meet all of the requirements of the continuing evaluation process.

C2.4.5.2. The primary consideration should be that the sum of the observation, both personal and through peer observation and reporting, is sufficiently detailed to allow for close evaluation of the individual.

C.2.4.5.3. Observation of performance and behavior need not be limited to duty in a single capacity. While observation of PRP duties should be primary, additional observation when not executing PRP duties as a government civilian employee, a private contractor to the government, a military service member or a combination of these can also serve to add to the certifying official's evaluation.

C2.4.6. After consulting with the CMA, determine reliability of individuals after medical evaluation/treatment *reveals PDI.*

C2.4.7. Remove individuals from PRP through appropriate action (suspension or decertification) as necessary based on the standards in this Regulation.

C2.4.7.1. For temporary decertification, advise the individual, in writing, of the reasons for temporary decertification within 15 workdays.

C2.4.7.2. For permanent decertification, advise the individual, in writing within 15 workdays, of the reasons for permanent decertification and of the requirement for review by the reviewing official.

C2.4.8. If applicable, ensure that contracts require contractor employees who perform duties in PRP positions under this Regulation meet the reliability standards of the PRP.

C2.4.9. Reevaluate designated PRP positions annually to determine the need for additional positions or the cancellation of unnecessary positions including contractor positions.

C2.5. COMPETENT MEDICAL AUTHORITIES (CMA)

C2.5.1. Provide the certifying official with sufficient medical information to make a sound judgment on an individual's suitability to perform PRP duties.

C2.5.2. Advise the certifying official and, when appropriate, the reviewing official, on all aspects of any condition that may reflect on an individual's suitability for assignment to a PRP position.

C.2.5.2.1. Notify the certifying official immediately of any condition classified in paragraph C5.1.6, Medical Condition.

C.2.5.2.2. Advise the certifying official of any medical condition, prescribed medication, or treatment that could detract from the ability of an individual in the PRP to perform assigned duties.

C2.5.3. Evaluate medical *and dental* records, perform further evaluation *and/or* medical examination, as necessary, ~~when a review is accomplished by other than the CMA and raises questions or identifies~~ *if* potentially disqualifying information about an individual's physical capability or mental suitability ~~for assignment to a PRP position~~ *is found*.

C2.5.4. In consultation with the certifying official, participate in continuing evaluation of PRP-certified individuals as described in Chapter 4 of this Regulation.

C2.6. SUPERVISORS

C2.6.1. Monitor the reliability of subordinates and notify the certifying official of any PDI.

C2.6.2. Be aware of how problems, concerns, and circumstances may reduce individual effectiveness and impair capability or reliability.

C2.7. INDIVIDUALS

C2.7.1. Be responsible for monitoring their own reliability and the reliability of others performing PRP duties. This is a 24 hours per day, 7 days per week responsibility. Failure to discharge these responsibilities may cast doubt on an individual's reliability.

C2.7.2. Be aware of how problems, concerns, and circumstances may reduce individual effectiveness and impair capability or reliability.

C2.7.3. Advise supervisors or the certifying official of any factors that could have an adverse impact on his/her performance, reliability, or safety while performing PRP duties.

C2.7.4. Inform support agencies of his/her active PRP status before treatment or consultation.

C2.7.5. Inform supervisors or the certifying official when another individual in the PRP appears to be involved in situations that may affect reliability.

C2.7.6. When a PRP-certified individual receives any type of *has received non-military* medical or dental treatment and/or evaluation (including TRICARE and Civilian Health and Medical Program of the Uniformed Services referrals) *that may impact performance or reliability*, he or she will report treatment and/or evaluation to the *CMA and/or* certifying official and. *Additionally, the individual will* provide appropriate documentation, *when available,* to the CMA, who shall consult the certifying official, *if required*.

C2.7.7. Personnel considered for or holding PRP positions shall make all medical records available to the CMA *to the appropriate designated individuals* for initial and subsequent screening requirements and for inspection.

C2.8. CONTRACTOR PROCEDURES

Certifying officials for contractors whose duties are subject to the PRP shall ensure that contracts require that the contractor employees performing duties in PRP positions under this Regulation shall meet the reliability standards of the PRP. Specifically, the contractor shall:

C2.8.1. Instruct managerial, supervisory personnel, medical personnel, and other support agencies and offices on the purpose, standards, and procedures of the PRP.

C2.8.2. Inform and instruct each employee of the significance of the assignment, PRP standards, the need for reliable performance, and the individual's responsibility for self-reporting and peer review of factors and situations that could adversely affect job performance or reliability.

C2.8.3. Ensure the individual presents a positive attitude toward the PRP and performing nuclear weapon duties and understands that maintaining PRP standards is a condition of continued employment in a PRP position.

C2.8.4. Ensure that employees to be assigned to a PRP position are subjected to a PSI, medical record evaluation, substance abuse testing, personal interview, proficiency certification, and continuing evaluation according to the certifying official, under the reliability standards of the PRP. Contractor personnel assigned to designated NC2 PRP positions shall be subject to random CSP testing.

C2.8.5. Provide the certifying official with results of a PSI, CSP (if required), medical record evaluation, and substance abuse testing of any contractor employee assigned, or proposed to be assigned, to a PRP position. Immediately report any other information about an employee not maintaining the reliability standards of the PRP.

C2.8.6. Provide for the continuing evaluation of employees assigned to PRP positions by contractor supervisory personnel, except when such employees are assigned to a DoD Component under the direct oversight of DoD personnel where the certifying official shall be responsible for that function.

C2.8.7. Remove an employee from a PRP position when notified by the certifying official that the employee has been suspended or decertified and notify the certifying official immediately of the removal action, and follow-up in writing within 15 *work*days. Suspension or temporary decertification from PRP duties requires that the employee be:

C2.8.7.1. Instructed to cease performance of PRP duties. Removal from PRP duties does not constitute a determination that the employee lacks necessary emotional or mental stability or physical capability to perform duties properly. It does indicate that there is a question about the employee's suitability that warrants restriction from PRP duties until the question is resolved.

C2.8.7.2. Prevented from entering any facility that would allow the individual access to areas containing nuclear weapons, and the employee's entry credentials shall be confiscated or deleted from the system.

C2.8.7.3. Removed from a PRP position on notification by the certifying official that the employee has failed to meet PRP reliability standards and has been permanently decertified. That action shall be reported to the Defense ~~Industrial Security Clearance Office (DISCO) (see subparagraph 2.8.8) and made a matter of permanent record by DISCO.~~ *Security Service (DSS) as an adverse action report through the DoD designated personnel security information system of record.*

C2.8.8. ~~Provide a current list of all contractor employees assigned to PRP positions to the DISCO, P.O. Box 2499, Columbus, OH 43216-5006. The list shall include employee name and~~

~~SSN; name and address of employer; and certifying official name, address and phone number.~~ *Use the DoD designated personnel security information system of record to record all employees assigned to PRP.*

C2.8.9. Comply with all other applicable areas of this Regulation.

C3. CHAPTER 3

CERTIFICATION

C3.1. GENERAL

C3.1.1. The certifying official shall confirm an individual's eligibility before that individual begins performing PRP duties. Certification and the individual's acknowledgment of understanding of his/her responsibilities while PRP certified shall be formally documented and maintained while the individual is performing PRP duties.

C3.1.2. The certifying official shall make a judgment on the reliability of each individual identified for PRP duties. This will be based on the appropriate personnel security investigation, physical and mental capability, review of personnel and medical records, position qualification requirements, and a personal interview.

C3.1.3. The certifying official shall consider all relevant facts applicable to the individual's performance record, the results of the PSIs and medical evaluations, and the opinions of other agencies and personnel, as appropriate, to make the final judgment about an individual's reliability and whether he or she can be depended on to respond in a stable manner when performing PRP duties. The qualifying criteria and processes described in this chapter shall be used by the certifying official in making that judgment.

C3.2. QUALIFYING CRITERIA

C3.2.1. Standards. The following represent the reliability standards expected of all PRP members:

C3.2.1.1. Physical competence, mental alertness, and technical proficiency commensurate with duty requirements.

C3.2.1.2. Dependability in accepting responsibilities and effectively performing in an approved manner; flexibility in adjusting to changes in the working environment, including ability to work in adverse or emergency situations.

C3.2.1.3. Good social adjustment, emotional stability, personal integrity, sound judgment, and allegiance to the United States.

C3.2.1.4. Positive attitude toward nuclear weapons duty, to include the purpose of the PRP.

C3.2.2. Personnel Security Investigation (PSI). An investigation required for determining the eligibility of DoD military and civilian personnel, contractor employees, consultants, and other persons affiliated with the Department of Defense, for access to classified information, acceptance or retention in the Armed Forces, assignment or retention in sensitive duties, or other designated duties requiring such investigation. PSIs include investigations of affiliations with subversive organizations, suitability information, or ~~hostage~~ *foreign preference and/or influence* situations conducted to make personnel security determinations. They also include investigations of allegations that arise subsequent to adjudicative action and require resolution to determine an individual's current eligibility for access to classified information or assignment or retention in a sensitive position (see Reference (~~e~~/)).

C3.2.3. Medical Evaluation. *The DoD Components shall specify procedures for individual health record information review. For the purposes of PRP, Reference (l) authorizes disclosure of protected health information of military personnel without authorization and of civilians and contractor employees pursuant to valid authorization.* Screening of medical and dental records must be performed by a CMA or other medical personnel specifically trained and formally designated to perform that function. When the *records* review is accomplished by other than the CMA and raises a question or identifies potentially disqualifying information about an individual's physical capability or mental suitability for assignment to a PRP position, the records shall be referred to the CMA for further evaluation or medical examination. The results of that review by the CMA along with all PDI shall be provided to the certifying official who shall make the determination on the individual's eligibility to perform PRP duties.

C3.2.4. Personnel File Review. The individual's personnel file, other official records, and information locally available on behavior or conduct about the individual's reliability shall be reviewed in detail. Look for evidence of the individual's acceptance of responsibility, exercise of sound judgment, effective performance, and ability to adjust to changes in the working environment. Personnel records shall reflect assignment of an individual to a PRP position.

C3.2.5. Personal Interview. A personal interview shall be conducted by the certifying official with each candidate for PRP duties. The personal interview shall not be conducted as a part of a routine orientation briefing for new personnel. PDI will be sought and, if appropriate, discussed during this interview.

C3.2.6. Position Qualification. Demonstrate potential for technical proficiency commensurate with nuclear weapon and/or NC2 duty position requirements.

C3.3. INITIAL CERTIFICATION

C3.3.1. Personnel Security Investigation and Eligibility Requirements

C3.3.1.1. Critical Position. Top Secret eligibility based on an SSBI, ~~or~~ SSBI-PR, *Phased Periodic ~~Review~~ Reinvestigation (PPR), or Tier 3 Investigation* completed *within the last 5 years* and *favorably* adjudicated ~~within the last 5 years~~. If appropriate, a review of the results of the investigation shall be conducted by the certifying official. If it becomes necessary to consider an individual for a critical position and the required investigation has not been completed, interim certification may be made (see paragraph C3.4).

C3.3.1.2. <u>Controlled Position</u>. ~~Secret eligibility based on a NACLC, ANACI, or SPR completed and adjudicated within the last 5 years or a favorably adjudicated SSBI, SSBI PR, SBI, SBI PR, BI, BI PR within the last 5 years.~~ *Secret eligibility based on a NACLC, ANACI, Secret Periodic Reinvestigation (SPR), SSBI, SSBI-PR, PPR, Special Background Investigation (SBI), SBI-PR, Background Investigation (BI), BI-PR, or Tier 2 Investigation completed within the last 5 years and favorably adjudicated.* If it becomes necessary to consider an individual for a controlled position and the required investigation has not been completed, interim certification may be made (see paragraph C3.4).

C3.3.1.3. <u>Fulfilling Investigative Requirements</u>

C3.3.1.3.1. Periodic reinvestigations are required every 5 years for both critical and controlled positions. Investigations determined to meet PRP position requirements under previous guidance remain valid.

C3.3.1.3.2. New Federal Investigative Standards issued by the Security Executive Agent, Office of the Director of National Intelligence, and the Suitability Executive Agent, Office of Personnel Management (Reference (p)) will replace the traditional PR with a "Continuous Evaluation/Reinvestigation" process. Until these new standards are implemented, agencies will continue to use the existing investigative standards in Director of Central Intelligence Directive 6/4 (Reference (q)) until the planned implementation date.

C3.3.1.4. The *DoD Components* may establish procedures to facilitate the timely screening of individuals required to support their wartime missions. Cost effectiveness should be considered in the implementation of *DoD Component* programs.

C3.3.2. <u>Medical Evaluation</u>

C3.3.2.1. As part of the required screening process, medical histories and records, if they are sufficiently comprehensive and current for the purpose, shall be evaluated to determine the candidate's physical and mental qualifications under the standards for the PRP. Personnel considered for or holding PRP positions shall make all medical records available to the certifying official for initial and subsequent screening requirements and for inspection. ~~See paragraph C3.3.2.1.3 below for restrictions on access to medical records for certifying and reviewing officials.~~

C3.3.2.1.1. Screening of medical records must be performed by a CMA or other medical personnel specifically trained and formally designated to perform that function. When the *records* review is accomplished by other than the CMA and raises a question or identifies potentially disqualifying information about an individual's physical capability or mental suitability for assignment to a PRP position, the records shall be referred to the CMA for further evaluation or medical examination. The results of that review by the CMA along with all PDI shall be provided to the certifying official who shall make the determination on the individual's eligibility to perform PRP duties.

C3.3.2.1.2. If available medical records are inadequate, the CMA shall conduct an evaluation to determine medical qualification under PRP standards. That medical evaluation shall include a mental health consultation when indicated. All PDI of a medical nature shall be documented in the individual's medical records.

C3.3.2.1.3. PRP certifying and reviewing officials are partially authorized to review medical records of candidates and members of the PRP to make determinations required by this Regulation. According to Reference (g), DoD medical records may be disclosed to reviewing and certifying officials for this purpose without either a request from, or the consent of, the individuals to whom those records pertain. PRP certifying and reviewing officials may only have access to portions of the medical records where the CMA has identified a possible disqualifying condition. Access is limited to the extent necessary for the certifying or reviewing official to document the condition to make a certification/qualification determination for PRP purposes. All PDI of a medical nature shall be documented in the individual's medical records.

C3.3.2.1.4. *C3.3.2.1.3.* Because of the sensitive and confidential nature of the records, *access* shall extend only to the reviewing and certifying officials and designated *PRP* inspectors *(see DL.34) consistent with Reference (l).* Such review shall be conducted with the assistance of a healthcare provider who can advise on medical record data that might otherwise be misinterpreted. See paragraph C3.3.2.1.3. for restrictions on access to medical records for certifying and reviewing officials.

C3.3.3. <u>Personnel File Review</u>. The individual's personnel file, other official records, and information locally available on behavior or conduct about the individual's reliability shall be reviewed in detail. Look for evidence of the individual's acceptance of responsibility, exercise of sound judgment, effective performance, and ability to adjust to changes in the working environment.

C3.3.4. <u>Personal Interview</u>. A personal interview by the certifying official shall inform the individual of the significance of the assignment, PRP standards, the need for reliable performance, the individual's responsibility for self-reporting and peer review of factors and situations that could adversely affect job performance or reliability. The certifying official will also provide the individual the opportunity to disclose any PDI.

C3.3.5. <u>Proficiency Qualification</u>. It shall be certified that the individual has had the formal course of instruction and/or possesses the minimum level of experience required for assignment to a particular critical or controlled PRP position.

C3.3.6. <u>Potentially Disqualifying Information</u> (PDI). Central Adjudication Facilities for military and DoD civilians or the DISCO *DSS* for contractor personnel, will forward all PDI, as defined in Chapter 5 of this Regulation, on PRP individuals to the appropriate certifying official/security manager. The certifying official will review this information and determine if the individual's reliability is affected and take appropriate actions. PDI previously addressed, documented, and determined not to be disqualifying for PRP assignment need not be re-addressed or require additional documentation unless warranted by subsequent disqualifying information. *The appropriate certifying official/security manager shall record a servicing relationship within the DoD designated personnel security information system of record and indicate the appropriate contact information so that the adjudication facility knows the appropriate location to send PDI.*

C3.4. INTERIM CERTIFICATION

C3.4.1. <u>Critical Position</u>. If it becomes necessary to consider an individual for a critical position and the required investigation has not been completed, interim certification may be made under the following conditions:

C3.4.1.1. For interim critical certification, the individual must have either Secret eligibility based on *an investigation* completed ~~and adjudicated investigation~~ within the last 5 years *and favorably adjudicated,* or Top Secret eligibility based on *an investigation* completed ~~and adjudicated investigation~~ no more than 10 years ago and *favorably adjudicated,* without a break in active Federal service or employment longer than 2 years.

C3.4.1.2. The SSBI *or Tier 3* request shall have been submitted prior to interim certification and all other requirements of the PRP screening process shall have been fulfilled.

C3.4.2 <u>Controlled Position</u>. If it becomes necessary to consider an individual for a controlled position and the required investigation has not been completed, interim certification may be made under the following conditions:

C3.4.2.1. For interim controlled certification, the individual must have ~~clearance~~ *Secret* eligibility based on an investigation ~~which has been~~ completed *within the last 10 years* and *favorably* adjudicated ~~within the last 10 years~~ without a break in service over 2 years.

C3.4.2.2. The NACLC, ANACI, ~~or~~ SPR *or Tier 2* shall have been submitted prior to interim certification and all other requirements for the PRP screening process shall have been fulfilled.

C3.4.3. <u>Individuals with Interim Certification</u>

C3.4.3.1. These individuals shall be identified to supervisory personnel, entry controllers who directly control access to exclusion areas, and others as necessary, as having only interim certification. Entry authorization lists and individual access media shall be specifically marked to designate interim certification status.

C3.4.3.2. An individual with interim certification shall not be paired in a two-person team with another individual also having only an interim PRP certification.

C3.5. PERSONNEL TRANSFER

C3.5.1. <u>PRP-certified Individual</u>. When a PRP-certified individual is transferred to another PRP position, he or she must be interviewed by the new certifying official. If this transfer does not involve a change in the reviewing official, a rescreening of the medical and personnel records is not required. If this transfer results in a change of both certifying and reviewing officials, a rescreening of the medical and personnel records shall be conducted.

C3.5.2. <u>PDI</u>. PDI previously addressed, documented, and determined not to be disqualifying for PRP assignment need not be re-addressed or require additional documentation unless warranted by subsequent disqualifying information.

C4. CHAPTER 4

CONTINUING EVALUATION

C4.1. GENERAL

Certifying officials are responsible for ensuring that all military, civilian, and contractor personnel assigned to PRP positions meet all of the requirements of the continuing evaluation process. Certifying officials must also observe the behavior and performance of members certified under the PRP on a frequent and consistent basis. The primary consideration for certifying officials should be that the sum of the observation, both personal and through peer observation and reporting, is sufficiently detailed to allow for close evaluation of the individual. Observation of performance and behavior need not be limited to duty in a single capacity. While observation of PRP duties should be primary, additional observation when not executing PRP duties as a government civilian employee, a private contractor to the Government, a military service member, or a combination of these can also serve to add to the certifying official's evaluation.

C4.2. MINIMUM STANDARDS

Members whose permanent duty assignments do not permit routine observation/peer reporting on a day-to-day basis must be monitored with particular diligence. For those personnel whose normal duties or assignments do not provide for routine observation (excluding periods of administrative absence (leave/pass/temporary duty, TDY, or TAD)), certifying officials must demonstrate an ability to maintain an equivalent level of confidence in the reliability of those members as would be available through routine, day-to-day contact and peer reporting. Individuals certified under PRP must be aware and agree that certain information/materials concerning their activities (medical, mental health, police, employment records, credit reports, etc.) both on- and off-duty, are to be provided for review voluntarily to certifying officials, CMAs, and inspectors and that failure to provide the requested materials may result in suspension or decertification.

C4.2.1. Certification for personnel who do not meet the requirements for routine observation as described above, but who the certifying official believes should be certified, require evaluation and approval by the Commander of the Combatant Command or the respective Chief of the Military Service or designated representative. The approval authority may be delegated in writing to a single official of at least O-7/SES grade on the staff. All exceptions will be submitted for review on a quarterly basis to ATSD(NCB)/NM. The certifying official will submit a specific plan outlining the application of the tools outlined in paragraph C4.2.2., tailored to the circumstances of the individual being considered that provides for the equivalent level of confidence mentioned above. This provision does not apply to the certification of certifying officials, who must meet the minimum standards for continuing evaluation in paragraph C4.2.

C4.2.2. For periods in which a PRP-certified individual was not subject to continuing evaluation, the certifying official must ensure the individual's reliability during these times meets the requirements of this Regulation. The certifying official will employ additional means and methods sufficient to assist in that determination, e.g., an additional personal interview, periodic medical records review, additional drug screening, contact with civilian employer of Selected Reserve personnel or previous supervisor, service/personnel records review, periodic criminal records/history checks, and credit checks. When selected randomly for drug screening, personnel will be required to submit to testing upon return to duty.

C4.3. PSI

All civilian, contractor, active duty military, and Selected Reserve personnel assigned to PRP positions shall be subject to a PR every 5 years, according to Reference (e/). The following applies:

C4.3.1. Personnel assigned to serve in PRP positions will have a PSI PR submitted every 5 years regardless of when they were last certified into the PRP.

C4.3.2. A break in Federal service or Government employment exceeding 2 years, and, for contractor employees a break in status exceeding 2 years.

C4.3.3. The certifying official may request a new PSI based on significant derogatory information or allegations.

C4.3.4. Reference (p) will replace the traditional PR with a "Continuous Evaluation/Reinvestigation" process. Until these new standards are implemented, agencies will continue to use the existing standards in Reference (q) until the planned implementation date. Once implemented the new frequency is:

C4.3.4.1. At least 20 percent of subjects in Tier 2 appointed to positions that require eligibility for access to "L" information, Confidential information, and Secret information shall be reevaluated annually, with 100 percent being reevaluated at least once every 5 years and on an a periodic basis or as event-driven, subject to implementing guidance.

C4.3.4.2. Subjects in Tier 3 appointed to positions that require eligibility for access to "Q" information, Top Secret information, or SCI shall be reevaluated annually or as event-driven, subject to implementing guidance.

C4.4. MEDICAL EVALUATION

C4.4.1. Each time a PRP-certified individual receives a medical evaluation and/or treatment that may impact performance or reliability, the CMA must determine PRP reliability effects and, if warranted, make recommendations to the certifying official. IDCs on submarines that are underway will ensure the certifying official is apprised of any medical treatment that might affect PRP performance and upon return to homeport, the CMA will review all treatment which could potentially impact PRP performance. Additionally, the ~~Services~~ *DoD Components* are authorized to establish protocols that may be applied by IDMTs at Munitions Support Squadrons and by IDCs on submarines that do not require CMA review. When an individual's duty performance may be impaired by medical care or the use of prescribed medication, as determined by the CMA, the certifying official shall be notified to decide if the individual shall be suspended from duty involving nuclear weapons for the period of medical care or use of medication.

C4.4.2. The certifying official shall be notified immediately by the CMA when a significant effect on the individual's physical or mental abilities is expected or if an individual's behavior indicates emotional instability, drug or alcohol abuse, or the need for treatment with narcotics, sedatives, tranquilizers, or other drugs that could impair perception or performance. If an individual's reliability is not in question, the certifying official shall assess the individual's condition, obtain a medical evaluation of the potential effects of any medication or treatment that may have been prescribed or purchased over-the-counter, discuss with the individual the previous effects of such medication or treatment, if appropriate, and then decide if either suspension, decertification, or return to PRP duties is appropriate. If there is a doubt or disagreement among healthcare providers about an individual's reliability, the certifying official shall be notified and provided sufficient information to make the final PRP determination.

C4.4.3. When a PRP-certified individual ~~receives any private,~~ *has received* non-military medical or dental treatment and/or evaluation (including TRICARE ~~and Civilian Health and Medical Program of the Uniformed Services~~ referrals) *that may impact performance or reliability*, he or she will report treatment and/or evaluation to the *CMA or* certifying official ~~and~~. *Additionally, the individual will* provide appropriate documentation, *when available,* to the CMA, who shall consult the certifying official *if required*.

C4.4.4. Because of the danger to public health and safety or to U.S. national security that might result from the failure of an individual performing PRP duties to perform reliably, mandatory substance abuse testing of all military, civilian, and contractor personnel assigned to PRP duties shall be conducted according to DoD Directives 1010.1 and 1010.9 (References (~~k~~*r*) and (~~l~~*s*)).

C4.4.5. Hypnosis shall not be administered to individuals certified under the PRP without the knowledge of the individual's certifying official. The certifying official shall evaluate the underlying reason for seeking hypnosis and the potential impact on performance, reliability, or safety while performing PRP duties. When screening an individual for PRP duties who has been administered hypnosis, the CMA shall determine if there was an underlying medical reason for the individual to seek hypnosis.

C4.5. CRIMINAL INVESTIGATIONS

Actions taken shall depend on the nature of the allegations and the sensitivity of the individual's PRP duties. After careful review of all the information, the certifying official may suspend, decertify, or allow the individual under investigation to continue in PRP duties. In making that determination, nuclear surety shall be the primary consideration and shall not be compromised to aid an investigation. Regardless of the status of the investigation, when nuclear surety is determined to be in jeopardy, the certifying official shall immediately remove the individual from the PRP.

C4.6. CONTRACTOR PRP CONTINUING EVALUATION

Contractor employees who have been determined eligible by the contract monitor and have been assigned to PRP positions shall be *annotated in the DoD designated personnel security information system of record or* identified to ~~DISCO~~ *DSS*, ~~P.O. Box 2499~~ *2780 Airport Drive, Suite 400*, Columbus, Ohio ~~43216-5006~~ *43219-2268*. On receipt of any information that may affect the reliability and trustworthiness of a contractor employee under the PRP, ~~DISCO~~ *DSS* shall forward that information to the appropriate certifying official.

C5. CHAPTER 5

DISQUALIFICATION, REMOVAL, AND REINSTATEMENT

C5.1. POTENTIALLY DISQUALIFYING OR DECERTIFYING CRITERIA

Any of the following traits or conduct may be grounds for disqualification or decertification of individuals from the PRP. In evaluating such traits or conduct, certifying and reviewing officials shall ensure there is no reasonable doubt of an individual's reliability and that it is in the best interest of national security that the individual be assigned to duties involving nuclear weapons. *If potential clearance eligibility impact is determined, the information will be provided to the appropriate CAF or for contractor employees, to DSS.*

C5.1.1. Alcohol. Any alcohol-related incident, alcohol abuse, or alcohol dependency (see DL.4, DL.5, and DL.6) may be grounds for removal or disqualification from PRP duties. The certifying official, after consultation with the CMA, shall determine the degree to which an alcohol problem impacts the reliability of the individual being considered for PRP assignment.

C5.1.1.1. Alcohol-Related Incident. Individuals involved in an alcohol-related incident shall be, at a minimum, suspended from PRP duties. The certifying official shall conduct an investigation of the circumstances and request a medical evaluation. If the individual is not returned to PRP duties within 120 days, temporary or permanent decertification actions shall be taken, as appropriate. Individuals prescribed an alcohol awareness/training class may be returned to PRP duties prior to completion of the class when the certifying official determines the individual to be reliable based on the results of an investigation and medical evaluation.

C5.1.1.2. Alcohol Abuse. Individuals diagnosed as alcohol abusers, but who are not diagnosed as alcohol dependent, shall, at a minimum, be temporarily decertified. Those individuals may have their temporary decertification removed and be returned to PRP duties after successfully completing a prescribed rehabilitation program or treatment regimen, when they have displayed positive changes in job reliability and lifestyle, and receive a favorable medical prognosis by the CMA. Failure to satisfactorily meet these requirements shall result in permanent decertification.

C5.1.1.3. Alcohol Dependency. Individuals diagnosed as alcohol dependent shall be disqualified or decertified from the PRP.

C5.1.1.3.1. Individuals temporarily decertified for alcohol dependency may have their temporary decertification removed and be returned to PRP duties after successfully completing rehabilitation, and a minimum of 180 days of a formal aftercare program according to DoD Instruction 1010.6 (Reference (aa)). A PRP qualification screening, to include a favorable prognosis by the CMA, shall be completed before rescreening or recertification.

C5.1.1.3.2. Failure to satisfactorily complete a formal aftercare program or other alcohol-related misconduct shall result in permanent decertification or disqualification.

C5.1.1.3.3. Any individual who voluntarily consumes alcohol after being diagnosed as alcohol dependent shall, at a minimum, be suspended from PRP duties. The certifying official, after consultation with the CMA, shall determine the degree to which the alcohol consumption impacts the reliability of the individual being considered for PRP assignment. If the individual is not returned to PRP duties within 120 days, temporary or permanent decertification actions shall be taken, as appropriate.

C5.1.1.4. Pre-Service (Alcohol-Related Incidents). Involvement in pre-service alcohol-related incidents, to include underage alcohol use which resulted in legal action, does not automatically render an individual ineligible for consideration for, or retention in, a PRP position. It is incumbent on the certifying official to determine the degree to which the alcohol related incidents impact the reliability of the individual being considered for PRP duties.

C5.1.2. Drugs. Drug abuse or drug dependency (see DL.21, DL.22.) is grounds for disqualification or decertification. A drug-related incident (see DL.23) is grounds for removal from PRP duties. The certifying official, after consultation with the CMA, shall determine the degree to which drug use impacts the reliability of the individual being considered for PRP assignment.

C5.1.2.1. Drug-Related Incident. Individuals involved in a drug-related incident shall be, at a minimum, suspended from PRP duties. Suspension under these circumstances shall only be used when reliability is not in question. The certifying official shall conduct an investigation of the circumstances and request medical evaluation. If the certifying official has any reason to doubt or suspect the individual's reliability for PRP duties the following actions will be taken:

C5.1.2.1.1. The individual concerned shall immediately be temporarily decertified.

C5.1.2.1.2. A complete evaluation shall be conducted of the individual's drug involvement and current and past duty performance.

C5.1.2.1.3. A PRP qualification re-screening including a complete medical evaluation shall be started.

C5.1.2.1.4. Removal of the temporary decertification and recertification into the PRP shall require thorough justification and documentation for recommendation for retention in PRP duties, a determination that recertification is in the best interest of the service and national security, and statements by the reviewing and certifying official that the individual's reliability is not in doubt.

C5.1.2.1.5. Individuals determined to be ineligible for recertification to PRP duties shall be permanently decertified, and that action shall be made a matter of permanent record, where applicable, such that the person cannot move to another location/unit and seek PRP certification.

C5.1.2.1.6. Any individual found to have been involved in the unauthorized trafficking, cultivating, processing, manufacturing, or sale of any controlled or illegal drug, to include cannabis-based products, shall be ineligible for PRP duties.

C5.1.2.1.7. Any individual found to have ever used a drug that could cause flashbacks (hallucinogens such as LSD, mescaline, etc.) is ineligible for PRP duties. In addition, any individual who has ever used peyote is ineligible for PRP duties, including those individuals otherwise protected under ~~Public Law 103-344 (42 U.S.C.~~ *section* 1996a~~)~~ *of title 42, U.S.C.* (Reference (~~au~~)).

C5.1.2.1.8. It is not the intent of this Regulation to automatically disqualify or decertify any individual from PRP who, in an effort to self-medicate, inadvertently or deliberately exceeds the recommended safe dosage on the medication's packaging of over-the-counter substances or who improperly uses prescribed medications. If the certifying official suspects or the individual admits to such improper usage, the individual must be suspended from PRP duties and the CMA consulted. If a CMA diagnosis of drug abuse is rendered, the certifying official shall permanently decertify the individual.

C5.1.2.2. <u>Drug Abuse</u>. Any individual diagnosed as a drug abuser will not be certified into the PRP or, if certified, will be permanently decertified, and those actions will be made a matter of permanent record such that the person cannot be transferred to another location/unit and become PRP certified.

C5.1.2.3. <u>Drug Dependency</u>. Any individual diagnosed as drug dependent will not be certified into the PRP or, if certified, will be permanently decertified, and those actions will be made a matter of permanent record such that the person cannot be transferred to another location/unit and become PRP certified.

C5.1.2.4. <u>Pre-Service Drug Use</u>. Pre-service use of marijuana, hashish, or other cannabis-based product does not necessarily render an individual ineligible for consideration for, or retention in, a PRP position. It is incumbent on the certifying official, with CMA consultation, to determine the degree that the pre-service drug use impacts the reliability of the individual being considered.

C5.1.2.4.1. It is not the intention of this Regulation to render automatically ineligible for the PRP all individuals who are or have been in the program after disclosing pre-Service or in-Service cannabis use and who, before May 25, 1993, were certified according to the PRP certification rules of their ~~Service~~ *DoD Component* that were in effect at the time of their first certification in which this use was considered during the PRP certification process. Further, if individuals were certified at a time when the Services did not require disclosure of cannabis use, and they subsequently made such disclosure, this disclosure will not be the sole reason for decertification.

C5.1.2.4.2. If the pre-Service cannabis use is discovered after an individual is already certified, and there is no other information that would cause doubt about the individual's reliability, the certifying official, with CMA consultation, may retain the individual in the PRP.

C5.1.3. <u>Other Substances</u>. Use of any other substances that alter perceptions or mental faculties including sniffing glue or aerosol fumes, shall be handled as drug incidents, abuse or dependence, respectively, as determined after consultation with the CMA.

C5.1.4. <u>Negligence or Delinquency in Performance of Duty</u>. If the certifying official's review of the PRP candidate's or certified member's job or duty history reveals a lack of dependability, flexibility, good attitude or good judgment, the member should not be certified, or should be decertified. In determining reliability, the certifying official must evaluate all aspects of an individual's actions.

C5.1.5. <u>Conviction of, or Involvement in, a Serious Incident</u>. Conviction by a military or civil court of a serious offense, including both felonies and misdemeanors, or involvement in a serious incident, or a pattern of behavior or conduct that is reasonably indicative of a contemptuous attitude toward the law or other duly constituted authority.

C5.1.6. <u>Medical Condition</u>. Any significant physical or mental condition substantiated by the CMA to be prejudicial to reliable performance of the duties of a particular critical or controlled position. The certifying official shall take the necessary actions to ensure that the individual is properly screened both medically and psychologically. Individuals who experience personal trauma, including but not limited to such events as family illness/death, violent crime, to include sexual assault or accidental injury, may experience psychological symptoms that impact reliability. When individuals affected by personal trauma seek medical care, the CMA will assess potential impact upon reliability, and advise the CO accordingly. The CMA is not required to disclose the personal circumstances that resulted in traumatization, but are required to inform the CO of the specific medical/psychological diagnosis and treatment that may potentially impact reliability. As with all potentially disqualifying medical conditions, the certifying official must decide each case on the specific medical and other pertinent evaluations of the individual involved. The primary consideration in all determinations must be in the best interest of national security.

C5.1.7. <u>Poor Attitude or Lack of Motivation</u>. Poor attitude or lack of motivation as evidenced by aberrant attitude or irrational behavior, inappropriate behavior or mood may be grounds for decertification.

C5.1.8. <u>Suicide Attempt and/or Threats</u>. Any suicide attempt and/or threat may be grounds for disqualification or decertification. In determining reliability, the certifying official must evaluate all aspects of the individual's action. Any suspected attempt and/or threat of suicide will result in the individual's temporary decertification from PRP duties pending the results of a mental health assessment/evaluation.

C5.1.9. <u>Loss of Confidence</u>. If for any reason the certifying official loses trust or confidence in a member's ability to perform PRP duties, the certifying official shall decertify the member.

C5.2. SUSPENSION

Suspension is used to immediately remove a member from PRP duties without starting decertification action. When suspended, a member is still considered reliable for the PRP, but because of the circumstances, is not authorized to perform PRP duties. Although a recommendation to suspend an individual from PRP duties may come from many sources, the certifying official must evaluate the situation and determine whether suspension is appropriate.

C5.2.1. Suspension shall be used only when the individual's reliability is not in question, when the problem is expected to be of short duration, and while conducting an investigation or medical evaluation to determine if a situation or incident could have an adverse effect on an individual's reliability.

C5.2.2. A suspension requires that the certifying official remove the individual from duties requiring PRP certification, notify the individual and his or her supervisor of the nature and circumstances about the suspension. A suspension will initially be for up to 30 days. However, the certifying official may extend the period of suspension up to 120 days in 30-day increments, when there is insufficient information to either remove the suspension or return the individual to PRP duties or to either temporarily or permanently decertify the member. If the issue cannot be resolved, or if the cause of the suspension lasts longer than 120 days, the individual shall be temporarily decertified until the issue is resolved and the individual is either returned to PRP duties or permanently decertified.

C5.3. DECERTIFICATION

Any individual who fails to meet the reliability standards specified in this Regulation shall not be assigned to, or continued in, duties of a PRP position. PRP certification shall be revoked immediately on a certifying official's determination that an individual no longer meets the standards in this Regulation. The certification shall terminate administratively when an individual transfers from a PRP position to one not requiring certification. There are two types:

C5.3.1. Temporary Decertification

C5.3.1.1. Temporary decertification from PRP duties shall occur immediately on receipt of information that is, or appears to be, a reason for decertification from the PRP. That action shall be taken when the certifying official has information that could be expected to affect an individual's job performance or reliability and suspension is not appropriate. Temporary decertification shall not be used if the facts dictate permanent decertification. When temporarily decertified, the individual may not perform PRP duties. Within 15 workdays of the temporary decertification, the certifying official shall provide the individual in writing the reason(s) for temporary decertification unless the individual is returned earlier to PRP duties. Individuals temporarily decertified will remain under continuous evaluation for PRP purposes until permanently decertified or returned to PRP duties.

C5.3.1.2. The certifying official shall investigate all information essential to a decision about revoking the temporary decertification or invoking a permanent decertification. During suspected alcohol or drug abuse, the investigation shall include a medical evaluation by the CMA.

C5.3.1.3. Temporary decertification shall not normally exceed 270 days. However, the certifying official may extend the period of temporary decertification in 30-day increments to a maximum of 365 days. Extensions shall be documented.

C5.3.2. <u>Permanent Decertification</u>. Individuals who the certifying official determines to no longer meet the reliability standards specified in this Regulation shall be permanently decertified. Within 15 workdays of the determination, the certifying official shall advise the individual, in writing, of the reasons for decertification and of the requirement for review by the reviewing official.

C5.3.2.1. Any of the following four conditions shall result in permanent decertification or, if an individual is being considered for a PRP position, permanent disqualification:

C5.3.2.1.1. An individual who is diagnosed as alcohol dependent and subsequently fails the required aftercare program.

C5.3.2.1.2. An individual who is diagnosed as a drug abuser.

C5.3.2.1.3. An individual who is diagnosed as drug dependent.

C5.3.2.1.4. An individual's security clearance is revoked.

C5.3.2.2. To ensure uniform application of the reliability standards specified by this Regulation and effective use of personnel, consistent with the purpose of the PRP, a reviewing official shall review each case involving a permanent decertification decision. The reviewing official may seek additional information or explanations of extenuating circumstances from the certifying official, the CMA, personnel officials, and the individual concerned, if appropriate.

C5.3.2.3. Following the review of the permanent decertification action, the reviewing official shall notify the individual and the certifying official of the findings and conclusion within 15 workdays. In the case of a DoD contractor employee, the contractor shall be told only that the employee has been decertified and must be reassigned to non-PRP duties in compliance with contractual requirements.

C5.3.2.4. If the reviewing official approves the permanent decertification, the individual shall be removed from positions requiring PRP certification and the action shall be made a matter of permanent record.

C5.4. REINSTATEMENT/REQUALIFICATION

C5.4.1. A certifying official or reviewing official may request reinstatement of a member's PRP certification or requalification consideration for members who were permanently decertified/disqualified provided the reason or condition of the permanent decertification or ineligibility no longer exists. Approval authority for reinstatement is Head of a DoD Component. Each Head of a DoD Component shall determine delegation authority within their Component. Requests for reinstatement or requalification must be in writing, contain justification and information as determined by Service directives. If reinstatement or requalification is approved, initial qualification/screening shall be completed as described earlier in this Regulation.

C5.4.2. Individuals permanently disqualified or decertified for alcohol dependency may be reinstated/requalified for PRP duties under the following conditions:

C5.4.2.1. The individual has successfully completed an initial intensive rehabilitation, according to Reference (m/).

C5.4.2.2. The individual has completed a 1-year period of strict compliance with aftercare program requirements according to Reference (m/).

C5.4.2.3. In all cases a PRP qualification screening including a favorable prognosis by the CMA and a psychological evaluation shall be completed before requesting reinstatement.

C5.4.2.4. The responsible certifying official must determine that the value of the member's continued presence in the PRP outweighs the risk from potential future alcohol-related incidents and must document the fact that he or she has full trust and confidence in the member's reliability.

AP1. <u>APPENDIX 1</u>

<u>PRP POSITIONS</u>

AP1.1. GENERAL

The reliability standards established in Chapter 3 shall be used to determine an individual's eligibility for a PRP position. All PRP positions shall be formally designated as either critical or controlled and shall be restricted to the minimum number required to accomplish the mission. Only certified personnel shall be assigned to designated PRP positions and when PRP positions become vacant, certified personnel shall be assigned as rapidly as possible. Examples of typical PRP positions are shown in Table AP1.T1., below.

AP1.2. REVIEW OF PRP POSITIONS

Certifying officials shall re-evaluate designated PRP positions annually to determine the need for additional positions or the cancellation of unnecessary positions.

AP1.3. PRP POSITION ELIGIBILITY

Eligibility for assignment to PRP positions, subject to the reliability standards in Chapter 3, shall be confirmed in writing by a certifying official. Before an individual is assigned to PRP duties, it shall be certified that the individual has had the required PSI and clearance, been screened according to the reliability standards, been personally interviewed by the certifying official, and been found eligible and qualified for assignment to a PRP position.

Table AP1.T1. PRP Positions

(This matrix is provided to assist in identifying PRP positions.)

Duty Position	Duty Position Example	PRP Designation
1. Commanders		
a. Delivery units	Navy submarine, Air Force wing - group, and squadron; persons delegated to act for the above on nuclear weapon operations.	Critical
b. Nuclear support units	Strategic Weapons Facilities, Air Force munitions or missile maintenance squadron.	Critical
2. Missile and air crews		
a. Delivery aircraft; missile crew	Pilots, navigators, and bombardiers; weapon system officers; electronic system officers; missile crewmembers.	Critical
b. Transport aircraft		
(1) With access	Self-explanatory	Controlled
(2) Without access	Self-explanatory	None
3. Delivery unit personnel and supervisors		
a. With access and technical knowledge	Persons who by the nature of their assigned duties could cause the unauthorized launch, release, or firing of a nuclear weapon.	Critical
b. With access, no technical knowledge	Handling, transporting, and launch personnel.	Controlled
c. Without access	Support such as clerks, cooks.	None
4. Nuclear support unit personnel and supervisors		
a. With access and technical knowledge	Persons who perform modifications, retrofits, limited life component changes, and similar tasks.	Critical
b. With access, no technical knowledge	Handling, transporting, and launch personnel.	Controlled
c. Without access	Support personnel such as clerks, cooks.	None
5. Handling and transport personnel	Vehicle operator, crane operators.	Controlled

6. Command disablement management team		
a. With access and technical knowledge	Personnel tasked with coding and/or recoding and/or checking built-in Command Disable System and external controlled Command Disable.	Critical
b. With access, no technical knowledge	Command Disablement Team.	Controlled
7. Delivery system maintenance personnel and supervisors		
a. With access and technical knowledge	Persons who could cause the unauthorized launch, release, or firing of a nuclear weapon.	Critical
b. With access, no technical knowledge		Controlled
c. Without access		None
8. Custodial unit personnel		
a. Custodians	(Reference (d)) Commander of a US custodial unit.	Critical
b. Custodial agents	(Reference (d)) Individuals acting on behalf of and for the custodian in maintaining control of access to US nuclear weapons and maintaining control of weapons prior to release.	Controlled
9. Explosive ordnance disposal (EOD)		
a. With access and technical knowledge	EOD technicians.	Critical
b. Without access	EOD technicians not assigned to PRP billets; EOD support such as clerks and mechanics.	None
10. Security Forces		
a. General	See DoD Directive 5210.41 (Reference (ev)).	
(1) Escort	Persons controlling access to weapons during transport.	Controlled
(2) Convoy	Convoy commanders, security escorts, and entry controllers to areas containing nuclear weapons during ground transport.	Controlled
(3) For Nuclear Command & Control (NC2) aircraft	Persons controlling access to occupied or locked NC2 aircraft with Positive Control Material present.	Controlled

(4) Augmenters		
(a) Armed	Persons routinely assigned to duties directly for nuclear weapon security who are armed and assigned to duties protect and guard a nuclear weapon or, when joined, the delivery system.	Controlled
	Persons assigned to the follow-on backup forces.	None
(b) Not armed	Persons not routinely assigned to nuclear weapon security duty, who are not armed, and not assigned duties to protect and guard a nuclear weapon or, when joined, the delivery system.	None
b. Army		
(1) Access control personnel	Entry control personnel and security guards directly controlling access to material access and exclusion areas.	Controlled
(2) Alarm monitors	Persons controlling and monitoring primary and redundant intrusion detection system.	Controlled
(3) Security force on-site commanders	Full-time member of the security force, assigned to Army nuclear support mission, who is on site with the authority and capability to direct physical protection activities and security response forces under emergency situations.	Controlled
(4) Armed guards	Armed personnel specifically assigned duties to protect and guard Army nuclear support mission.	Controlled
(5) Security response forces	Armed security personnel assigned to installations with an Army nuclear support mission but not directly assigned to day-to-day guard duties.	None
c. Navy/Marine Corps		
(1) Security forces afloat		
(a) Internal and inside of perimeter	Persons who control entry into an exclusion area; includes permanently assigned guards and personnel assigned and stationed to support a submarine exclusion area.	Controlled
(b) Alarm monitors	Persons who control primary and redundant intrusion detection system's annunciation equipment.	Controlled
(c) Response Forces		

<u>1</u>. Armed initial response forces	Reaction Forces assigned Reaction Force direct support duties. Persons assigned to the Security Response Team.	Controlled
<u>2</u>. Armed augmentation forces	Reaction Forces assigned support duties. Persons assigned to the Backup Alert Force, Reserve Force and Augmentation Force ~~(AF)~~.	None
(2) Security forces ashore		
(a) Internal and inside perimeter	Persons who control entry into waterfront restricted area, exclusion area or limited area; includes permanently assigned guards in any such area.	Controlled
(b) Alarm monitors	Persons who control primary and redundant intrusion detection system's annunciation equipment.	Controlled
(c) External to perimeter	Persons permanently ordered and solely dedicated to nuclear weapons security duties who are armed and specifically assigned duties to protect and guard a nuclear weapon or, when joined, the delivery system.	Controlled
(d) Escort	Persons controlling access to weapons during transport.	Controlled
~~(e) Augmenters (Reserve and Backup Force (RF/BF))~~		
~~<u>1</u>. Armed~~	~~Persons routinely assigned to duties directly for nuclear weapon security, meeting the requirements of security who are armed and assigned duties to protect and guard a nuclear weapon or, when joined, the delivery system.~~	~~Controlled~~
~~<u>2</u>. Armed or unarmed~~	~~Persons not routinely ordered to duties directly for nuclear weapon support of nuclear weapons security are considered to be in support. This support post provides BF capability to any location of the base or region wherein it is assigned.~~	~~None~~

d. Air Force		
(1) Inside restricted areas and at close-in or exclusion areas	Permanently assigned security forces posted in these areas to guard nuclear weapons and control entry to the areas. Includes entry controllers, Security Response Team, Fire Teams, Response Force, Camper Alert Team, Security Escort Team, area supervisor, etc.	Controlled
(2) Security system operators and administrators, security controllers (C3), and ICBM flight security controllers	Security forces personnel who operate, monitor, or administer primary, remote and/or redundant nuclear area or facility electronic security systems, integrated security systems, or subsystems. Security personnel who provide primary command, control, and communications (C3) for nuclear weapon security operations.	Controlled
(3) Convoy	Convoy commanders, security escorts, and entry controllers to areas containing nuclear weapons during ground transport.	Controlled
(4) Lethal denial system operators	Primary, alternate, or remote operators of lethal denial systems dedicated to nuclear weapon security.	Controlled
(5) Keys and codes	Persons who maintain, account for, and issue keys, codes, and combinations that provide access to nuclear weapons.	Controlled
(6) Security augmenters routine	Includes support forces or units, security augmentees, National Guard and Reserve Forces. Armed persons assigned nuclear security duties in USAF restricted areas on a routine or permanent basis.	Controlled
11. Nuclear weapon inspectors		
a. With access	Position equal to that being inspected.	Critical or controlled
b. Without access		None
12. Personnel in command and control line	Persons who control or use authenticators and/or emergency action messages; PAL teams and; PAL and other coded control devices teams; staff officers, contractors and other personnel who control or use strategic or tactical nuclear-certified computer data.	Critical May also be specially designated personnel – (See position example 14 below.)

13. **Communications security personnel**	Persons who receive and distribute sealed authenticators, PAL material, or related codes.	Critical
14. **Designated NC2 personnel**	Personnel with access to NC2 coding and authentication processes and a communications medium necessary to transmit release, execution, or termination orders; personnel involved in the preparation and production of NC2 coding and authentication documents and equipment; personnel involved in preparation and production of nuclear weapons targeting tapes and materials; and other personnel who could have an adverse impact on system performance for nodes and equipment that represent near-single-point-failure elements for the NC2 system.	Critical

AP2. APPENDIX 2

PRP ANNUAL STATUS REPORT

Each DoD Component maintaining a PRP shall provide an annual program status report to the ATSD(NCB/NM) by February 15 of the following year. The annual status report shall include, for the preceding calendar year ending December 31, PRP certification and permanent decertification statistics by component and category of personnel (e.g., Air Force (military); Federal and/or DoD civilian; and active duty, Selected Reserves, or defense contractor). A recommended format is provided below.

DoD Nuclear Weapon Personnel Reliability Program Annual Status Report

Calendar Year Ending December 31, 2XXX

DoD Component:_____

Total number of PRP certified personnel

	U.S.		Europe		Pacific		Total	
	Critical	Controlled	Critical	Controlled	Critical	Controlled	Critical	Controlled
Active Duty Military								
Guard/Reserves								
Civilians								
Contractors								

~~Total number of PRP interim certified personnel~~

	~~U.S.~~		~~Europe~~		~~Pacific~~		~~Total~~	
	~~Critical~~	~~Controlled~~	~~Critical~~	~~Controlled~~	~~Critical~~	~~Controlled~~	~~Critical~~	~~Controlled~~
~~Active Duty Military~~								
~~Guard/Reserves~~								
~~Civilians~~								
~~Contractors~~								

Total number of personnel pending investigation/adjudication for PRP assignment

	U.S.		Europe		Pacific		Total	
	Critical	Controlled	Critical	Controlled	Critical	Controlled	Critical	Controlled
Active Duty Military								
Guard/Reserves								
Civilians								
Contractors								

Total PRP permanent decertifications

	U.S.		Europe		Pacific		Total	
	Critical	Controlled	Critical	Controlled	Critical	Controlled	Critical	Controlled
Active Duty Military								
Guard/Reserves								
Civilians								
Contractors								
Reason for permanent decertifications								
Alcohol-Related								
Active Duty Military								
Guard/Reserves								
Civilians								
Contractors								
Drug-Related								
Active Duty Military								
Guard/Reserves								
Civilians								
Contractors								
Negligence or delinquency in performance of duty								
Active Duty Military								
Guard/Reserves								
Civilians								
Contractors								
Conviction by a military or civilian court of a serious offense; a pattern of behavior or conduct indicative of a contemptuous attitude toward the law or other duly constituted authority								
Active Duty Military								
Guard/Reserves								
Civilians								

	U.S.		Europe		Pacific		Total	
	Critical	Controlled	Critical	Controlled	Critical	Controlled	Critical	Controlled
Contractors								
Any significant physical or mental condition substantiated by a competent medical authority; aberrant behavior considered by the certifying official as prejudicial to reliable duty performance in a PRP critical or controlled position								
Active Duty Military								
Guard/Reserves								
Civilians								
Contractors								
Poor attitude or lack of motivation								
Active Duty Military								
Guard/Reserves								
Civilians								
Contractors								
Suicide attempt or threat								
Active Duty Military								
Guard/Reserves								
Civilians								
Contractors								
Loss of confidence								
Active Duty Military								
Guard/Reserves								
Civilians								
Contractors								

Total number of personnel granted requalification or reinstatement to PRP assignment

	U.S.		Europe		Pacific		Total	
	Critical	Controlled	Critical	Controlled	Critical	Controlled	Critical	Controlled
Active Duty Military								
Guard/Reserves								
Civilians								
Contractors								